Homemade Gifts

Nicki Trench

Homemade Gifts

Easy techniques and great projects

COLLINS & BROWN

First published in the United Kingdom in 2009 by
Collins & Brown
10 Southcombe Street
London
W14 0RA

An imprint of Anova Books Company Ltd

Distributed in the United States and Canada by
Sterling Publishing Co, 387 Park Avenue South,
New York, NY 10016-8810, USA

ISBN 978-1-84340-531-3

A CIP catalogue for this book is available from
the British Library

10 9 8 7 6 5 4 3 2 1

Reproduction by Mission Productions, Hong Kong
Printed and bound in China
By 1010 Printing International Ltd

This book can be ordered direct from the
publisher at www.anovabooks.com.

Contents

Introduction

Homemade is enjoying a revival. The time and effort spent making someone a gift is far more appreciated, enjoyable and cost-effective than simply handing over cash at the till for a ready-made gift. The high street is not the inspiring place it once was – independent shops full of interesting delights have been taken over by chains and what gifts are left are often unoriginal. In the time taken to park and fight your way through hordes of shoppers, you could easily have made one of the delightful gifts in this book.

You don't have to be the perfect knitter, cook, or homemaker to make the gifts in Homemade Gifts. The patterns and recipes are simple and clear, some with step-by-step instructions to help you along the way. Whether you're a beginner or an expert, you'll find the projects enormously satisfying to make. This is an inspirational book that will appeal to everyone who appreciates the revival of all things homemade.

Strawberry Tea Cosy

The art of tea-making is back and once you have made up this tea cosy a tea pot will look naked without it. This makes a fantastic gift, especially when combined with a gorgeous packet of tea or a pretty mug. The cosy is worked using the yarn double throughout, which thickens up the sides to keep your tea steaming hot.

Strawberry Tea Cosy

Size
To fit a standard 4–6 cup teapot

Materials
- Two 50g balls of Rooster Almerino Aran 310 Rooster Red (A)
- One 50g ball of Rooster Almerino Aran Cornish 301 (B) and Gooseberry 306 (C)
- One pair of 6mm knitting needles

Tension
13 stitches and 18 rows to 10cm (4in) over stocking stitch using 6mm needles and yarn double

Abbreviations

Alt:	alternate
Dec:	decrease
Foll:	following
Inc:	increase
K:	knit
K2 tog:	knit two stitches together
P:	purl
Psso:	pass slipped stitch over
P2 tog:	purl two stitches together
Rem:	remaining
RS:	right side
Skpo:	slip one stitch, knit one stitch, pass slipped stitch over
St st:	stocking stitch
St/sts:	stitch, stitches
WS:	wrong side

Sides (both alike)
With A double, cast on 24 sts.
Work in garter st for 2 rows, ending after a WS row.
Join in B double.
Stranding yarn not in use loosely across WS of work, weaving it in every 2 or 3 sts, cont in patterned st st as follows:-

Row 3 (RS): With A inc in first st, with B k1, [with A k3, with B k1] five times, with A k1, inc in last st. *26 sts*

Row 4 and every foll alt row to row 28: With A, purl.

Row 5: With A, inc in first st, knit to last st, inc in last st. *28 sts*

Row 7: With A inc in first st, with B k1, [with A k3, with B k1] six times, with A k1, inc in last st. *30 sts*

Row 9: With A, knit.

Row 11: With A k4, [with B k1, with A k3] six times, with B k1, with A k1.

Row 13: With A, knit.

Row 15: With A k2, [with B k1, with A k3] seven times.

Row 17: With A, knit.

Row 19: With A k2tog, k2, [with B k1, with A k3] six times, with A k2tog. *28 sts*

Row 21: With A, k2tog, knit to last 2 sts, k2tog. *26 sts*

Row 23: With A k4, [with B k1, with A k3] five times, with B k1, with A k1.

Row 25: With A, knit.

Row 27: With A k2, [with B k1, with A k3] six times. Break off B and cont using A double only.

Row 28: Purl.

Row 29: [K2tog] three times, knit to end. *23 sts*

Row 30: [P2tog] three times, purl to end. *20 sts*

Rows 31 and 32: As rows 29 and 30.

Cast off rem 14 sts.

Leaves (make 4)

With C double, cast on 3 sts.

Row 1 (RS): Knit. Inc in first st, p1, inc in last st. *5 sts*

Row 3: Knit.

Row 4: Inc in first st, p3, inc in last st. *7 sts*

Row 5: Knit.

Row 6: P2tog, p3, p2tog. *5 sts*

Row 7: Knit.

Row 8: P2tog, p1, p2tog. *3 sts*

Row 9: Knit.

Row 10: Slip 1 st, p2tog, psso and fasten off.

Stalk

With C double, pick up and knit 1 st from centre of cast-on edge of each Leaf. *4 sts*

Starting with a purl row, work in st st until stalk measures 3cm (1¼in) from pick-up row, ending after a purl row.

Next row: [K2tog] twice, slip these sts back onto left needle and, without turning work and pulling yarn quite tightly across WS of work, work across these 2 sts again as follows:- skpo and fasten off.

To make up

Press carefully following instructions on ball band. Join Sides together along row-end and cast-off edges, leaving 8cm (3¼in) opening in one side seam (for handle) and 7cm (2¾in) opening in other side seam (for spout). Attach Leaves and Stalk to top of Tea Cosy using the photograph on page 10 as a guide.

Chutney

There is nothing better or more wholesome than homemade chutney. Plum chutney is best if you use fresh fruit from the garden and chilli chutney has a real bite. Fill recycled jars with chutney and give generously to all your friends and family. A wonderful accompaniment to good cheeses or meats.

Plum Chutney

- 450g (1lb) red plums, halved and stoned
- 180g (6oz) caster sugar
- 120ml (4½fl oz) cider vinegar
- 1 cinnamon stick
- 2 star anise

Makes 1.35–1.8kg (3–4lbs)

Method

Put all the ingredients into a pan and heat gently until all the sugar has dissolved. Bring the mixture to the boil and simmer gently for about 20–30 minutes until the plums are tender and the liquid is syrupy. Bottle as described below.

General tips

Conversions are not exact, so use either metric or imperial meaures, but not a mixture of both. Wash all fruit before you use it. Sterilize the jars and lids by washing and drying them thoroughly and placing them in a warm oven (110ºC) for approx 15 minutes.

Bottling chutney

Pour the chutney into the hot, sterilized jars. Fill as full as possible as the mixture settles down into the jars. Cover each with a waxed sealing disc and seal with a tight lid. Label when cold.

Chilli Chutney

- 10–20 fresh red chillies
- Splash of olive oil
- 2 red onions, peeled and chopped
- Sprig of fresh rosemary
- 2 fresh bay leaves
- 5cm (2in) length of cinnamon stick
- Sea salt
- Fresh ground black pepper
- 100g (4oz) brown sugar
- 150ml (5fl oz) balsamic vinegar

Wear gloves when handling chillies.

Makes approx 3.6kg (8lbs)

Method

Place the chillies under a hot grill, turning until blackened and blistered. Place in a bowl and cover with clingfilm until cool. Peel off the skin, trim the stalks and scoop out the seeds, then chop finely. Heat the olive oil in a saucepan and add the onions, rosemary, bay leaves, cinnamon and seasoning. Cook slowly until the onions are rich, golden and sticky. Add the chopped chillies, sugar and vinegar and cook until it reduces to a thick sticky chutney. Remove the cinnamon and bay leaves and season well to taste. Bottle as described on page 14.

Wholesome homemade chutney is a definite crowd-pleaser.

Crochet Picnic Blanket

Home-made crocheted or knitted blankets are a
well-loved comfort zone in the home. This blanket is
the ultimate gift. A lovingly hand-crafted blanket
is a valued and treasured gift for any occasion.
Don't be daunted by the task of crocheting a large
blanket, this will be dissipated by completing
one square at a time that only takes a short while to
complete. They are ideal short tasks for making
during the evenings, or while you're waiting in the
school car park, on trains, planes... anywhere!

Crochet Picnic Blanket

Size

Finished size 146cm (57½in) x 122cm (48in)

Materials

- Twenty 50g balls of Rooster Almerino Aran in Ocean 309 (A)
- Seven 50g balls of Rooster Almerino Aran in Gooseberry 306 (B)
- Two 50g balls of Rooster Almerino Aran in each of Brighton Rock 307 (C), Strawberry Cream 303 (D), Cornish 301 (E) and Spiced Plum 308 (F)
- One 5.00mm crochet hook

Tension

One completed motif measures 12cm (4¾in) square using 5.00mm crochet hook

Abbreviations

dc = double crochet
ch = chain
ss = slip stitch
tr = treble
puff st= [yarn over hook and insert hook as indicated, yarn over hook and draw loop through, pulling loop up to 2.5cm (1in)] four times, yarn over hook and draw through all 9 loops on hook.

Motifs (Make 120)

Note: Colours C, D, E and F are used at random for centre of motifs.

With first centre colour, make 4 ch and join with a ss to form a ring.

Round 1 (RS): With first centre colour, 1 ch (does NOT count as st), 8 dc into ring, ss to first dc. *8 sts*
Fasten off.

Round 2: Join in second centre colour to same st as where first centre colour was fastened off, draw up a loop approx 2.5cm (1in) long, 1 puff st into same place as where yarn was rejoined, 3 ch, [1 puff st into next dc, 3 ch] seven times, ss to top of puff st at beg of round. *32 sts*
Fasten off.

Round 3: Join in B to one ch sp of round 2, 3 ch (counts as first tr), 3 tr into same ch sp, [5 tr into next ch sp, 4 tr into next ch sp] three times, 5 tr into last ch sp, ss to top of 3 ch at beg of round. *36 sts*
Fasten off.

Round 4: Join in A to same st as where B was fastened off, 3 ch (counts as first tr), miss st at base of 3 ch, 1 tr into each of next 5 tr, [3 tr into next tr, 1 tr into each of next 8 tr] three times, 3 tr into next tr, 1 tr into each of last 2 tr, ss to top of 3 ch at beg of round. *44 sts*
(Do not fasten off.)

Round 5: With A, 3 ch (counts as first tr), miss st at base of 3 ch, 1 tr into each of next 6 tr, [5 tr into next tr, 1 tr into each of next 10 tr] three times, 5 tr into next tr, 1 tr into each of last 3 tr, ss to top of 3 ch at beg of round. *60 sts*
Fasten off.

To make up

Lay out Motifs to form one large rectangle 10 Motifs wide and 12 Motifs long. When you are happy with the arrangement of the colours of the motif centres, join them together with crocheted seams. To join Motifs, hold them RS tog and work a line of dc along the edges to be joined, inserting hook through the edges of both Motifs. Join Motifs into strips first, then join the strips to form the final rectangle.

Edging

With RS facing, attach A to one st around outer edge of joined Motifs, 1 ch (does NOT count as st), work 1 round of dc around entire outer edge of joined Motifs, working 3 dc into each corner and ending with ss to first dc.
Fasten off.

Apron

This is such a fantastic present for someone who loves to cook and ideal for those who prefer a half apron. It's a very quick project to make and takes very little fabric. Choose material that might match the recipient's kitchen or favourite colours. Here we have used some gorgeous polka-dotted fabric in a duck egg blue.

Apron

Size

One size fits all

Materials

- 125cm (50in) length of 115cm (45in) wide fabric
- Sewing needle
- Thread to match fabric

Any cook will love this pretty half apron with its useful pocket at the front.

1) For the apron, cut one piece 78cm (30¾in) wide x 46cm (18in) long. For the straps, cut two pieces each 80cm (31½in) long x 8cm (3¼in) wide to tie at the back.

2) On one long edge of the main apron, turn over the raw edge once by approx 1cm (⅜in), then turn over again by approx 2cm (¾in) to make a double hem approx 3cm (1¼in) deep. Pin, stitch and press. Repeat this step on the other long edge.

3) Double hem the two remaining sides using the same method but making the hem narrower, approx 2cm (¾in) wide.

4) For the pocket, cut a piece of fabric 28cm (11in) wide x 21cm (8¼in) long. Fold over one long edge by 0.5cm (¼in) and then by 1cm (⅜in) to make a double hem at the top of the pocket. Pin and sew across. On the other three sides, fold under the edges once by 2cm (¾in). Press, pin and tack the folds in place.

5) Place the pocket onto the front of the apron in the centre, with the bottom edge 8cm (3¼in) up from the bottom. Pin in place. Sew around the three sides leaving the top open. Measure the pocket and place a marker pin at the top, middle and bottom down the centre line. Sew a straight line from top to bottom of the pocket to divide it into two sections. Remove tacking.

6) Fold one piece of strap fabric in half lengthways and press. Open it out flat and fold both long raw edges to the centre fold line. Press.

7) Fold the strap in half again, press, pin and then sew down one long side, just in from the open edge.

8) At one end, fold the raw edges of the strap inside and pin. Sew in place. Repeat on the other strap.

9) Fold in the other end of the strap in the same way and sew this end of the strap firmly in place at one end of the apron waistband. Repeat for the other strap.

Embroidered Tablecloth and Napkins

Even a very beginner will be able to make this tablecloth. It's an ideal project to give as a gift because it looks impressive, but takes only basic sewing knowledge. The tablecloth and napkins are hemmed in a straight line and the strawberry is embroidered using very simple and basic embroidery stitches.

Tablecloth and Napkins

Size
Tablecloth: to fit the table
Napkins: 33cm (13in) square

Materials
- Buy enough fabric to cover your table, allowing for an approx 25cm (10in) drop plus a 1.5cm (⅝in) seam allowance on each side. Depending on the width of the fabric that you buy, 75cm (30in) should be enough for about six napkins.
- Bobble trim: measure the length and the width of your tablecloth, add together and multiply by two to get the length of trim required
- Sewing needle
- Embroidery thread in red, green and white
- Embroidery hoop
- Embroidery needle
- Thread to match fabric and trim

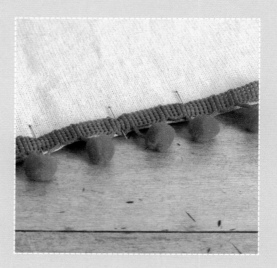

1) Measure your table and add 53cm (21¼in) to both the length and the width for the drop and the seam allowances all round. Cut the fabric to size. Cut six 36cm (14¼in) squares for the napkins.

2) Turn over the edges of the tablecloth by 0.5cm (¼in) and then by 1cm (⅜in), pin in place and then hem with a straight stitch. Repeat on the napkins. Press the hems.

3) Pin and sew bobble trimming around the edges of the tablecloth only.

4) Trace a suitable embroidery motif onto tracing paper. Turn the tracing paper over and draw around the lines on the back with a soft pencil. Turn the tracing paper the right way up again and position the motif in one corner of one of the napkins. Go over the lines again with a sharp pencil to transfer the design to the fabric of the napkin. Repeat on all napkins and in each corner of the tablecloth.

5) Hand embroider the motifs in each corner of the tablecloth and on one corner of each napkin. Here we have stitched strawberries to tie in with the bobble fringe, using a simple straight satin embroidery stitch with French knots for the pips.

Miss Bunny Rabbit

Miss Bunny is the cutest rabbit ever. She is an excellent gift for a newborn or a baby's birthday since she is knitted in stocking stitch, which makes her feel smooth and soft. Make her in a luxurious yarn such as Rooster's Almerino, which is a mix of supersoft Merino wool made from very soft fleece and alpaca fleece. Don't over-stuff, as Miss Bunny Rabbit is best quite squidgy.

Miss Bunny Rabbit

Size
Completed rabbit measures approx 35cm (13¾in) from tips of ears to tips of toes

Materials
- One 50g ball of Rooster Almerino DK in each of Hazlenut 202 (A) and Cornish 201 (B)
- Small amount of Rooster Almerino Aran in Brighton Rock 307 (C) (for embroidered spots on dress)
- Oddments of black and blue yarn (for embroidered facial features)
- One pair of 3.50mm knitting needles
- Washable toy filling

Tension
24 stitches and 30 rows to 10cm (4in) over stocking stitch using 3.50mm needles

Abbreviations
Inc:	increase
K:	knit
K3tog:	knit three stitches together
K2tog:	knit two stitches together
P2tog:	purl two stitches together
P:	purl
Rem:	remaining
Rep:	repeat
RS:	right side
St st:	stocking stitch
St(s):	stitch(es)
Tbl:	through back loop
WS:	wrong side

Body

With A, cast on 15 sts.
Starting with a knit row, work in st st throughout as follows:-
Work 2 rows.
Row 3: Inc in first st, [k1, inc in next st] rep to end. *23 sts*
Work 3 rows.
Row 7: K1, [inc once in each of next 2 sts, k1] seven times, k1. *37 sts*
Work 20 rows.
Row 28: Inc in first st, p to last st, inc in last st. *39 sts*
Work 2 rows.
Row 31: Inc in first st, [k18, inc in next st] twice. *42 sts*
Work 9 rows.
Row 41: K4, k3tog, [k4, k3tog] four times, k4, k2tog, k1. *31 sts*
Work 1 row.
Break yarn and thread through rem 31 sts. Pull up tight and fasten off securely. Join row-end edges (to form one side seam) and insert toy filling. Sew cast-on edges together, with side seam at one end of this base seam.

Head

With A, cast on 5 sts.
Starting with a knit row, work in st st throughout as follows:-
Work 2 rows.
Row 3: Inc once in each of first 2 sts, k1, inc once in each of last 2 sts. *9 sts*
Work 1 row.
Row 5: K1, [inc in next st, k1] four times. *13 sts*
Work 3 rows.
Row 9: Inc in first st, [k3, inc in next st] three times. *17 sts*
Work 5 rows.
Row 15: Inc in first st, k4, inc in next st, k5, inc in next st, k4, inc in last st. *21 sts*
Work 7 rows.

Divide for ears

Row 23: Cast off 1 st, knit to end. *20 sts*
Row 24: Cast off 1 st, purl until there are 9 sts on right needle and slip these 9 sts onto a holder (for second ear), cast off 1 st, purl to end.
**Work 18 rows on this set of 9 sts only for first ear.
Next row (RS): [K1, k3tog] twice, k1. *5 sts*
Next row: P2tog, p1, p2tog. *3 sts*
Break yarn and thread through rem 3 sts. Pull up tight and fasten off securely.**
Return to sts left on holder and rejoin yarn with RS facing. Complete second ear exactly as given for first ear from ** to **.

Join row-end edges of ear sections (to form inner seams of ears), then join row-end edges of head section. Insert toy filling, leaving ears ·empty. Sew cast-on edges together, with head seam at centre back of head. Using the photograph on page 30 as a guide, sew head to top of body.

Arms (make 2)

With A, cast on 5 sts.
Starting with a knit row, work in st st throughout as follows:-
Work 1 row.
Row 2: Inc once in each of first 2 sts, p1, inc once in each of last 2 sts. *9 sts*
Work 26 rows.
Row 29: K2tog, k5, k2tog. *7 sts*
Work 1 row.
Row 31: K2tog, k3, k2tog. *5 sts*
Work 1 row.
Row 33: K2tog, k1, k2tog. *3 sts*
Row 34: P3tog and fasten off.
Join row-end edges (to form underarm seam), then insert toy filling. Using the photograph on page 30 as a guide, sew cast-on edge to shoulder section of body.

Legs (make 2)

With A, cast on 9 sts.
Starting with a knit row, work in st st throughout as follows:-
Work 1 row.
Row 2: Inc once in each of first 2 sts, p5, inc once in each of last 2 sts. *13 sts*
Work 30 rows.
Row 33: K2tog, k9, k2tog. *11 sts*
Break yarn and thread through rem 11 sts. Pull up tight and fasten off securely.
Join row-end edges (to form inside leg seam), then insert toy filling. Using the photograph on page 30 as a guide, sew cast-on edge to base seam of body.

Dress front and back (both alike)

With B, cast on 29 sts.
Work in garter st for 4 rows.
Starting with a knit row, work in st st throughout as follows:-
Row 5: K6, k2tog tbl, knit to last 8 sts, k2tog, k6. *27 sts*
Work 5 rows.
Repeat last 6 rows three times more. *21 sts*
Row 29: K6, k2tog tbl, k5, k2tog, k6. *19 sts*
Work 1 row.

Shape armholes

Cast off 2 sts at beg of next 2 rows. *15 sts*
Row 33: K1, k2tog tbl, knit to last 3 sts, k2tog, k1. *13 sts*
Work 1 row.
Repeat last 2 rows once more. *11 sts*

Shape neck

Row 37: K1, k2tog tbl, k2 and turn, leaving rem 6 sts on a holder.
Work on this set of 4 sts only for first side of neck.
Work 1 row.
Row 39: K1, k2tog, k1. *3 sts*
Work 5 rows.
Cast off.
Return to sts left on holder and slip centre st onto a safety pin. Rejoin yarn to rem 5 sts with RS facing and cont as follows:-
Row 37: K2, k2tog, k1. *4 sts*
Work 1 row.
Row 39: K1, k2tog tbl, k1. *3 sts*
Work 5 rows.
Cast off.
Join right shoulder seam.

Neck edging

With RS facing and B, pick up and knit 9 sts down left side of front neck, knit st left on safety pin, pick up and knit 9 sts up right side of front neck, and 9 sts down right side of back neck, knit st left on safety pin, then pick up and knit 9 sts up left side of back neck. *38 sts*
Cast off knitwise (on WS).
Join left shoulder and neck edging seam.

Armhole borders (both alike)

With RS facing and B, pick up and knit 24 sts evenly all round armhole edge.
Cast off knitwise (on WS).

To make up

Rabbit

Using the photograph on page 30 as a guide, embroider facial features as follows:-
Using oddment of blue yarn, embroider two satin stitch eyes. Using oddment of black yarn, embroider straight stitch eyelashes above each eye, a round satin stitch nose, and a straight stitch mouth.

Dress

Join side and Armhole Border seams. Using the photograph on page 30 as a guide and C, embroider French knot 'spots' across dress at random.

Baby Chick Egg Cosies

An inspiring gift for Easter, these baby chicks have come to town ready to keep your eggs warm while you're cooking toasty soldiers. The egg cosies are very simple and you need only a basic knowledge of crochet, a small amount of yarn, a crochet hook and a piece of felt to create a little family of joy. The chicks also make perfect first projects to teach children how to crochet.

Baby Chick Egg Cosies

Size
To fit a standard hen's egg

Materials
- For chick, small amount of DK or soft aran weight yarn (A), such as Rowan Calmer in Refresh 487 (blue), Debbie Bliss Rialto DK in Yellow 07 (yellow), Debbie Bliss Cotton DK in 43 (green), Rooster Almerino Aran in Brighton Rock 3097 (pink) and Rowan Classic Cashsoft DK in Bella Donna 502 (lilac)
- For combs, small amount of Rowan Pure Wool DK in Kiss 036 (B)
- One 3.50mm crochet hook
- Oddments of felt in black (for eyes) and light pink, orange, dark pink, blue (for beaks)

Tension
18 stitches and 18 rounds to 10cm (4in) over double crochet fabric using 3.50mm crochet hook

Abbreviations
Ch: chain
Dc: double crochet
Dc2tog: [insert hook as indicated, yarn over hook and draw loop through] twice, yarn over hook and draw through all 3 loops on hook.
Rep: repeat
RS: right side
Ss: slip stitch
St(s):   stitch(es)

Chick egg cosy

With A, make 2 ch.
Round 1 (RS): 6 dc into 2nd ch from hook. *6 sts*
Round 2: [2 dc into next dc] six times. *12 sts*
Round 3: [2 dc into next dc] twelve times.
24 sts
Round 4: 1 dc into each dc to end.
Rounds 5 to 10: As round 4.
Round 11: [1 dc into next dc, dc2tog over next
2 dc] eight times. *16 sts*
Fasten off.

Comb

With B, make 8 ch.
Row 1: 1 dc into 4th ch from hook, [3 ch, 1 dc
into next ch] twice, 2 ch, miss 1 ch, 1 dc into last ch.
Fasten off.

To make up

Using the photograph on page 36 as a guide,
sew Comb to top of Egg Cosy. Cut tiny circles of
black felt and attach to front of Egg Cosy to
form eyes. From contrasting colour felt, cut out
a small diamond shape for beak and sew to
front of Egg Cosy between and below eyes –
attach diamond with a line of stitches across
the centre and fold felt in half along this
stitched line.

These simple baby chick egg cosies are the ideal
project to teach your children how to crochet.
Make them with any scraps of wool to hand – you
only need a tiny amount for each chick.

Father Christmas

A soft, knitted Father Christmas makes a fun gift to put in the top of a Christmas stocking and also fits really well at the top of the Christmas tree! He won't just be popular at Christmas time since he is just the right size to carry around. Take care not to stuff him too firmly as he should be soft and easy to handle when complete. He is knitted all in garter stitch – just knit stitch, no purl – to give him a nicely rounded and plump feel.

Father Christmas

Size
Completed toy measures approx 35cm (13¾in) from tip of hat to base of feet

Materials
- One 50g ball of Rowan Pure Wool DK in each of Scarlet 041 (A), Hay 014 (B), Anthracite 003 (C) and Enamel 013 (D)
- Oddment of blue yarn (for embroidered eyes)
- One pair of 4mm knitting needles
- Two small bells (optional – do not use if giving toy to a child under 3 years old)
- Washable toy filling

Tension
22 stitches and 40 rows to 10cm (4in) over garter stitch using 4mm needles

Abbreviations
Alt:	alternate
Dec:	decrease
Foll:	following
Inc:	increase
K:	knit
K2 tog:	knit two stitches together
Rem:	remaining
RS:	right side
St/sts:	stitch, stitches
WS:	wrong side

Body and Head

With A, cast on 44 sts.
Starting with a RS row, work in garter st throughout as follows:-
Work 28 rows.

Shape shoulders

Row 29 (RS): K9, [k2tog] twice, k18, [k2tog] twice, k9. *40 sts*
Work 1 row.
Row 31: K8, [k2tog] twice, k16, [k2tog] twice, k8. *36 sts*
Row 32: K7, [k2tog] twice, k14, [k2tog] twice, k7. *32 sts*
Row 33: K6, [k2tog] twice, k12, [k2tog] twice, k6. *28 sts*
Row 34: K5, [k2tog] twice, k10, [k2tog] twice, k5. *24 sts*
Break off A and join in B.
Work 1 row.

Shape chin

Row 36 (WS): K1, [inc in next st, k2] seven times, inc in next st, k1. *32 sts*
Row 37: K3, [inc in next st, k4] five times, inc in next st, k3. *38 sts*
Row 38: K3, [inc in next st, k5] five times, inc in next st, k4. *44 sts*
Work 16 rows.

Shape top of head

Row 55 (RS): K3, [k2tog, k4] six times, k2tog, k3. *37 sts*
Row 56: K4, [k2tog, k2] seven times, k2tog, k3. *29 sts*
Row 57: [K2tog, k2] three times, k2tog, k1, [k2tog, k2] three times, k2tog. *21 sts*
Row 58: [K2tog, k1] twice, [k2tog] three times, [k1, k2tog] three times. *13 sts*
Break yarn and thread through rem 13 sts. Pull up tight and fasten off securely. Join row-end edges to form centre back seam, leaving cast-on edge open. Insert toy filling.

Feet and legs feet (make 2)

With C, cast on 16 sts.
Starting with a RS row, work in garter st throughout as follows:-
Work 12 rows.
Break off C and join in B.
Work 2 rows.
Break off B and join in A.
Work 26 rows.
Cast off.

Boot cuff

With RS facing and C, pick up and knit 16 sts along 'ridge' worked in C.
Next row: [K1, inc in next st] eight times. *24 sts*
Work 2 rows.
Break off C and join in D.
Work 1 row.
Cast off.
Join row-end edges, leaving cast-off edge open, then join row-end edges of boot cuff. Insert toy filling. Positioning seam up inside of leg, sew cast-off edges of legs to cast-on edges of Body and Head, inserting a little more toy filling if required.

Arms [make 2]

With A, cast on 14 sts.
Starting with a RS row, work in garter st throughout as follows:-
Work 1 row.
Row 2: Inc in first st, k5, inc once in each of next 2 sts, k5, inc in last st. *18 sts*
Work 4 rows.
Break off A and join in D.
Work 2 rows.
Break off D and join in A.
Work 18 rows.
Row 27: K2tog, [k6, k2tog] twice. *15 sts*
Row 28: K2tog, k5, k2tog, k4, k2tog. *12 sts*
Row 29: K2tog, [k3, k2tog] twice. *9 sts*
Row 30: K2tog, k1, k2tog, k2, k2tog. *6 sts*
Row 31: [K2tog] three times. *3 sts*

Cast off.
Join row-end edges below row 27. Insert toy filling. Positioning seam underneath arm, sew arms to Body and Head at shoulder level.

Tunic skirt

With C, cast on 48 sts.
Starting with a RS row, work in garter st throughout as follows:-
Work 4 rows.
Break off C and join in A.
Work 12 rows.
Cast off.
Join row-end edges. Positioning seam at centre back, sew cast-on edge to Body and Head level with row 6 of Body.

Beard

With D, cast on 1 st.
Starting with a RS row, work in garter st throughout as follows:-
Inc 1 st at beg of next 21 rows. *22 sts*
Work 4 rows.
Row 26 (WS): K5 and slip these sts onto a holder, cast off next 12 sts, knit to end.
Work on this set of 5 sts only for first side of beard.
Dec 1 st at end of next and foll 2 alt rows. *2 sts*
Work 1 row.
Cast off.
Return to 5 sts left on holder and rejoin yarn with RS facing.

Dec 1 st at beg of next and foll 2 alt rows. *2 sts*
Work 1 row.
Cast off.
Using the photograph on page 40 as a guide,
sew beard to front of Head.

Moustache

With D, cast on 8 sts.
Row 1: Inc in first st, k6, inc in last st. *10 sts*
Row 2: Knit.
Row 3: [K5tog] twice. *2 sts*
Cast off.
Using photograph on page 40 as a guide, sew
moustache to front of Head above Beard.

Hat

With D, cast on 61 sts.
Starting with a RS row, work in garter st
throughout as follows:-
Work 3 rows.
Break off D and join in A.
Row 4: K1, [k2tog, k8] six times. *55 sts*
Work 3 rows.
Row 8: K1, [k2tog, k7] six times. *49 sts*
Work 3 rows.
Row 12: K1, [k2tog, k6] six times. *43 sts*
Work 3 rows.
Row 16: K1, [k2tog, k5] six times. *37 sts*
Work 3 rows.
Row 20: K1, [k2tog, k4] six times. *31 sts*
Work 3 rows.
Row 24: K1, [k2tog, k3] six times. *25 sts*

Work 3 rows.
Row 28: K1, [k2tog, k2] six times. *19 sts*
Work 3 rows.
Row 32: K1, [k2tog, k1] six times. *13 sts*
Work 9 rows.
Break yarn and thread through rem 13 sts.
Pull up tight and fasten off securely. Sew back
seam of hat. Using the photograph on page 40
as a guide, sew Hat to top of Head, folding up
first few rows at front of Head to form the
turn-up cuff.

To make up

Using the photograph on page 40 as a guide,
embroider facial features as follows:-
Using oddment of blue yarn, embroider French
knot eyes. Using A, embroider straight stitch
mouth between Beard and Moustache, and
satin stitch nose. Using D, embroider a square
of chain stitch on section of Tunic Skirt in C to
form buckle. Run gathering threads around
Arms next to stripe in D and pull up to form
wrist. Using D, make a 4cm (1½in) pompon and
attach to top of Hat. If required, attach bells to
front of boots as in photograph.

Love Your Cookies

Pretty iced heart-shaped cookies are a token of love. Use different coloured icing to cover the cookies and decorate with sparkly silver balls. These make gorgeous Wedding Day 'favours' to decorate the table. They can also be used as place settings if you pipe the guests' names on them using royal icing.

Love Your Cookies

Cookie base

- 1 medium free-range egg
- 50g (2oz) caster sugar
- 50g (2oz) soft brown sugar
- 75g (3oz) golden syrup
- 80g (3¼oz) butter
- 1 teaspoon mixed ground spices
- ¼ teaspoon bicarbonate of soda
- 375g (12oz) plain flour

Icing

- 250g (9oz) icing sugar
- Water
- Food colouring
- Edible silver balls

Makes approx 10 biscuits

Sweet melt-in-the-mouth hearts to delight the senses and show how much you care.

Cookies

Mix all the ingredients for the cookies in a food processor until the mixture forms a ball. If the mixture is too liquid add a little more flour, if it is too dry and crumbly add a few more drops of water. Wrap the ball of dough in a plastic bag and leave in the fridge for about an hour.

Pre-heat the oven to 180°C/350°F/Gas 4, line and grease a baking tray.

Roll out the dough on greaseproof paper until it is approx 1cm (³⁄₈in) thick.

Cut out heart-shaped cookies and place them onto the baking tray. Place in the oven and bake until the cookies have turned a golden colour (approx 20 minutes). Take the cookies out of the oven and allow to cool.

Icing

Mix the icing sugar with some water until the consistency becomes a loose paste. Divide the mixture into three bowls and add a different food colouring to each as required.

Using a knife or the back of a teaspoon, spoon a thin layer of icing onto the top of each cookie and smooth out.

Decorate each cookie with silver balls.

Make-up Bag

This fun and easy make-up bag takes up very little fabric, so is fantastic for using up those odd pieces of material that you have lying around. It's also a great opportunity to cut up old dresses in beautiful prints that you no longer wear but can't bear to part with. A make-up bag is an excellent gift, especially if you buy some items of make-up to put inside.

Make-up Bag

Size

Approx 20cm (8in) long x 10cm
(4in) high

Materials

- 2 pieces each 26 x 18cm
  (10½ x 7¼in) of main fabric for
  the outer bag
- 2 pieces each 26 x 18cm
  (10¼ x 7¼in) of lining fabric
- 17.5cm (7in) zip
- Sewing needle
- Thread to match fabric

1) With the main fabric pieces right sides
together, fold over 1.5cm (⅔in) along one long
edge on both pieces and press in place.

2) Open out the flaps again and tack the two
pieces together along the fold line. Open the
seam flat and press.

3) Place the zip on top of the opened out
seam in the centre. Make a chalk mark or
mark with a pin at each end of the zip, where
the zip teeth finish. Remove the zip from the
fabric and put aside.

4) Transfer the mark you just made to the wrong side of the seam allowance flaps.

5) With the flaps together, sew a short seam along the fold line from the edge of the fabric to approx 0.5cm (¼in) past the mark made in step 4. Repeat at the other end of the fold line.

6) Remove any pins. Open the fabric out flat, right side facing down, and press the seam allowance open.

7) Place the zip right side down on the centre of the seam allowance. The ends of the zip should slightly overlap the stitched sections of the seam made in step 5. Pin and tack the zip in place.

8) Remove any pins from the fabric. Turn the fabric over and, with the right side facing upward, take out the tacking stitches holding the seam together in the centre for around three-quarters of the length of the zip from the zip pull end.

9) Open the zip for around three-quarters of its length from the zip pull end.

10) Change the foot on your sewing machine for a zipper foot (if you have one). With the zip side facing upwards, sew the zip in place by sewing around all four sides. When you get to the zip pull, close it slightly to move it away from the needle so you don't have to stitch past it.

11) Take out the remaining tacking stitches and open the zip.

12) With the fabric right sides together, pin and sew the bottom and side seams.

13) Open out all the seams and press.

14) Put your hand into a bottom corner of the bag and open out the corner by spreading your fingers. Feel down with your other hand to match up the side and bottom seams at the corner. When one seam is directly on top of the other, place a pin across the corner to hold it in place.

15) Place the corner on a flat surface and measure 3cm (1¼in) down the seam line from the corner, then place a pin marker.

16) At the pin marker, using a ruler, mark the sewing line across the corner with tailor's chalk or pencil. It should be approx 7.5cm (3in) in length. Pin and sew along the marker line. Take out pins.

17) Repeat steps 14–16 on the other corner.

18) Trim off the excess fabric at the corners with pinking shears.

Lining

With the lining fabric right sides together, pin and sew the side and bottom seams, leaving the top open.

Repeat steps 13–18 as for the main fabric. Fold over the top edge by approx 1.5cm (²/₃in) and press.

Slip the lining inside the main piece, easing it in place carefully. Pin the top edge of the lining along the bottom of the zip, a short distance from the teeth. (Sometimes it's easier to turn the bag inside out to pin the lining in place.)

Hand stitch the top edge of the lining in place.

Patchwork Blanket

If you have a love for fabrics and can't stop yourself from buying pieces of old material, or if you have clothes that you simply can't throw away, patchwork is perfect for you – particularly in light of current trends for being thrifty and recycling. Start making a collection of 15cm (6in) squares – you will need 108 squares for a good size blanket, but make it bigger if you need it for a bed or a large sofa.

Patchwork Blanket

Size

Finished measurement approx
110 x 146cm (44 x 57in)

Materials

- 108 x 15cm (6in) squares of cotton
  fabric in various colours and prints
- 6m (232in) x 7cm (3in) wide ribbon
  or a strip of fabric this length
- 15cm (6in) patchwork template
  square
- 1.5m (60in) length of fleece to fit the
  finished size of blanket
- Sewing needle
- Thread to match the fabric

1) Press each piece of fabric before cutting
out 108 x 15cm (6in) squares, using the
patchwork template.

2) Lay out the squares on the floor or on a
large table and move them around to make
sure you haven't got two squares the same
next to each other.

3) Take two squares and, with right sides
facing, sew them together with a 0.5cm (¼in)
seam. Continue joining the squares together
in rows, until you have nine rows of nine
squares. Press all the seams open.

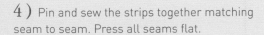

4) Pin and sew the strips together matching seam to seam. Press all seams flat.

5) Place the fleece fabric on a flat surface and push out creases. Lay the patchwork on top of the fleece, right side up, and pin the two layers together. Cut fleece to the same size as the blanket. Pin and sew the fleece to the patchwork as close to the edges as possible.

6) Using a hand sewing needle and thread, take a few stitches right through the fleece and the patchwork top in each corner of the squares. Pull the thread through several times and secure with a knot. This holds the fleece and the patchwork in place.

7) Fold the ribbon or strip of fabric in half. With the patchwork side of the blanket facing, pin the edging to the blanket with raw edges in line. Work in sequence by first pinning along one side, cutting the ribbon to length leaving a 3cm (1¼in) overlap. Repeat on the opposite side. Sew along both lengths close to the edge. Remove any remaining pins.

8) Fold the edging over the raw edge of the blanket and pin on the fleece side. Hand sew both strips of edging to the fleece.

9) Repeat on the remaining sides of the blanket. Trim and fold the corners of the edging neatly, then hand sew in place.

Birthday Blossom Cake

This pretty cake is perfect for a child's birthday cake. If you take the rabbit off and replace it with a bunch of candles, it's the ideal cake for any age and will delight everyone. The lemon cake in the middle just melts in your mouth and the blossoms are surprisingly easy to make. You can create your own colour scheme with the many edible dusts that are available in cake decorating shops.

Birthday Blossom Cake

Size

10cm (4in) deep cake (mixture will fill tin to the top)

Lemon cake

- 125g (4oz) butter
- 175g (6oz) caster sugar
- 175g (6oz) self-raising flour
- 1 teaspoon baking powder
- 2 extra large free-range eggs
- 4 tablespoons milk
- Finely grated zest of 1 lemon

Buttercream filling

- 125g (4oz) butter, softened
- 1 tablespoon milk
- 375g (12oz) icing sugar
- Confectioner's sugar (optional)
- Zest of 1 lemon and juice of
  ½ lemon

Cake icing

- 500g (20oz) white fondant icing
- Cornflour (for dusting)

Rabbit

- 30g (1¼oz) pale golden brown fondant icing (sugarpaste) for the body, arms, ears, head
- 7g (¼oz) white fondant icing (sugarpaste) for the tummy, muzzle, feet and tail
- Small amount pale pink fondant icing (sugarpaste) for the nose
- Sugar glue
- Black edible food colour for the eyes

Blossoms

- 250g (10oz) pot of Platinum Paste (Antique White) or Flower Paste
- Blossom cutter
- Edible dust in various colours
- Dust brushes
- Bone modelling tool
- Tweezers
- Confectioner's varnish

- Candle

Lemon cake

Pre-heat the oven to 180°C/350°F/Gas 4. Lightly grease a 10cm (4in) deep round cake tin and line with greased greaseproof paper. Measure all the cake ingredients into a large bowl or mixer and beat until well blended. Pour the mixture into the cake tin and level the surface. Place in the oven and bake for approx 35–40 minutes or until cooked. Test by lightly pressing the cake – if it springs back, it's cooked. Leave in the tin until cold, then turn out and remove the greaseproof paper.

Buttercream filling

Mix all the buttercream ingredients together to form a firm paste. Spread very thinly over the cake as a glue to stick the fondant icing.

Cake icing

Work the fondant icing for the cake until it is smooth and easy to handle. Dust a worksurface with cornflour. Roll the icing out into a circle large enough to cover the cake. Place it carefully and evenly over the cake. Dust your hands with cornflour and gently smooth the icing to the shape of the cake. Using a sharp knife, trim the bottom edges. To shine the surface, dust your hands with cornflour and rub gently over the fondant. Leave to dry overnight. (Do not refrigerate.)

Rabbit

Roll a long teardrop in pale brown fondant icing for the body. For the arms, roll sausage shapes with rounded ends. Flatten one end and make three cuts in the top. Stick the arms on the body with sugar glue. To make the head, roll a small amount into a ball and stick onto the body. Make two ears and indent down the centre of each with a cocktail stick. Stick in position, turning down the tip of one ear.

Divide the white paste into four pieces. With one, model a flattened teardrop for the tummy patch and stick in place with sugar glue. Use two more pieces to make the feet, cutting twice in the top to mark toes. Stick the feet in position. With the last piece, shape a flattened oval for the muzzle, marking the smile with a cocktail stick. Shape an oval of pink for the nose. Mark the eyes with black food colour. Sit the rabbit on top of the cake with the candle.

Blossoms

Roll the paste very thinly onto a board dusted with cornflour. Cut out blossoms, then colour using edible dust and a flat brush. Curl the petal edges by pressing down gently along the edge with a bone modelling tool. Use tweezers to dip each blossom into the confectioner's varnish, then leave to dry. When dry, stick each blossom onto the cake using sugar glue or royal icing.

Fingerless Mittens

Fingerless mittens are popular for men, women and teenagers. Once you make one pair for someone, it won't be long before you're asked to make another, and another... until you'll have learned the pattern by heart. Make these in either double knit or the thicker aran weight yarn, depending on how cold the weather is outside!

Fingerless Mittens

Size
Small (large)

Materials
- One 50g ball of Rooster Almerino Aran in each of Spiced Plum 308 (A), Strawberry Cream 303 (B) and Brighton Rock 307 (C)
  (Note: If making mittens in just one colour, one 50g ball is sufficient.)
- One pair each of 3.50mm and 4mm knitting needles

Tension
18 stitches and 26 rows to 10cm (4in) over stocking stitch using 4mm needles

Abbreviations

Alt:	alternate	Rep:	repeat
Inc:	increase	RS:	right side
K:	knit	Foll:	following
P:	purl	St(s):	stitch(es)

Left mitten
With 3.50mm needles and A, cast on 34 (36) sts.
Row 1 (RS): [K1, p1] rep to end.
Row 2: As row 1.
These 2 rows form rib.
Keeping rib correct, now work in stripes as follows:-
Join in B.
Using B, rib 2 rows.
Join in C.
Using C, rib 2 rows.
Last 6 rows form stripe sequence.
Keeping 6 row stripe sequence correct throughout, cont as follows:-
Work in rib for 8 rows more.
Change to 4mm needles.
Keeping stripe sequence correct and starting with a knit row, work in st st for 6 (8) rows.

Shape thumb gusset
Row 1 (RS): K15 (16), inc once in each of next 2 sts, k17 (18). *36 (38) sts*
Row 2 and every foll alt row: Purl.
Row 3: K15 (16), inc in next st, k2, inc in next st, k17 (18). *38 (40) sts*
Row 5: K15 (16), inc in next st, k4, inc in next st, k17 (18). *40 (42) sts*
Row 7: K15 (16), inc in next st, k6, inc in next st, k17 (18). *42 (44) sts*
Row 9: K15 (16), inc in next st, k8, inc in next st, k17 (18). *44 (46) sts*
Starting with a purl row, work st st for 7 rows.

Divide for thumb

Next row (RS): K27 (28) and turn, leaving rem 17 (18) sts on a holder.

Next row: Inc in first st, p11 and turn, leaving rem 15 (16) sts on holder.

Next row: Inc in first st, k12. *14 sts*

Starting with a purl row, work in st st on these 14 sts only for 3 (5) rows.

Now work in rib for 4 (5) rows.

Cast off in rib.

Join thumb seam.

Shape hand

Return to sts left on holder and slip first 17 (18) sts onto right needle, pick up and knit 2 sts from base of thumb, then knit across rem 15 (16) sts. *34 (36) sts*

**Starting with a purl row, work in st st across all sts for 7 (9) rows.

Work in rib for 5 (6) rows.

Cast off in rib.

Right mitten

Work exactly as given for Left Mitten to start of thumb gusset shaping.

Shape thumb gusset

Row 1 (RS): K17 (18), inc once in each of next 2 sts, k15 (16). *36 (38) sts*

Row 2 and every foll alt row: Purl.

Row 3: K17 (18), inc in next st, k2, inc in next st, k15 (16). *38 (40) sts*

Row 5: K17 (18), inc in next st, k4, inc in next st, k15 (16). *40 (42) sts*

Row 7: K17 (18), inc in next st, k6, inc in next st, k15 (16). *42 (44) sts*

Row 9: K17 (18), inc in next st, k8, inc in next st, k15 (16). *44 (46) sts*

Starting with a purl row, work in st st for 7 rows.

Divide for thumb

Next row (RS): K29 (30) and turn, leaving rem 15 (16) sts on a holder.

Next row: Inc in first st, p11 and turn, leaving rem 17 (18) sts on holder.

Next row: Inc in first st, k12. *14 sts*

Starting with a purl row, work in st st on these 14 sts only for 3 (5) rows.

Now work in rib for 4 (5) rows.

Cast off in rib.

Join thumb seam.

Shape hand

Return to sts left on holder and slip first 15 (16) sts onto right needle, pick up and knit 2 sts from base of thumb, then knit across rem 17 (18) sts. *34 (36) sts*

Complete exactly as given for Left Mitten from **.

To make up

Sew in all ends. Join side seams.

Baby Boy's Tank Top

You will be so much more appreciated if you knit something special for a newborn baby or for baby's first birthday. Hand-knitted gifts are often kept long after the baby has grown out of them and are often affectionately passed down to siblings. This stripey tank top is light, soft and easy to knit. Use natural wool that breathes and keeps the baby warm in winter and cooler in summer months.

Baby Boy's Tank Top

Size

To fit ages:

3–6 [6–9:9–12] months

Actual chest measurements:

55 (59:63)cm (21½ [23¼:24¾]in)

Length to shoulder:

25 [27:29]cm (9¾ [10½:11½]in)

Materials

- Two 50g balls of Rooster Almerino DK in each of Glace 205 (A) and Cornish 201 (B)
- One pair each of 3.75mm and 4mm knitting needles

Tension

21 stitches and 28 rows to 10cm (4in) over stocking stitch using 4mm needles

Abbreviations

Alt:	alternate
Cont:	continue
K:	knit
K2 tog:	knit two stitches together
P:	purl
Rem:	remaining
Rep:	repeat
RS:	right side
Skpo:	slip one stitch, knit one stitch, pass slipped stitch over
St st:	stocking stitch
St/sts:	stitch, stitches
WS:	wrong side

Back

With A and 3.75mm needles, cast on
58 (62:66) sts.
Row 1 (RS): K2, [p2, k2] rep to end.
Row 2: P2, [k2, p2] rep to end.
These 2 rows form rib.
Work in rib for 4 rows more.
Change to 4mm needles, join in B.
Starting with a knit row, now work in st st in
stripes as follows:-
With B, work 4 rows.
With A, work 4 rows.
These 8 rows form striped st st and are
repeated throughout.
Cont in striped st st until back measures 13
(14:15)cm (5 [5½:6]in), ending after a purl row.

Shape armholes

Keeping stripes correct, cast off 6 sts at beg of
next 2 rows. *46 (50:54) sts***
Next row: K2, skpo, knit to last 4 sts, k2tog, k2.
44 (48:52) sts
Next row: Purl.
Rep last 2 rows three (four:five) times more.
38 (40:42) sts
Cont straight until armhole measures
12 (13:14)cm (4¾ [5:5½]in), ending after a
purl row.

Shape shoulders

Cast off 9 (10:10) sts at beg of next 2 rows.
Break yarn and leave rem 20 (20:22) sts on
a holder.

Hand-knitted gifts are often treasured long after
the baby has grown out of them. This cute tank top
may well become a family heirloom.

Front

Work exactly as given for Back to **.

Divide for neck

Row 1 (RS): K2, skpo, k14 (16:18), k2tog, k2, turn, leaving rem 24 (26:28) sts on a holder. Work on this set of 20 (22:24) sts only for first side of neck.

Row 2: Purl.

Row 3: K2, skpo, knit to last 4 sts, k2tog, k2. *18 (20:22) sts*

Rep rows 2 and 3 two (three:four) times more. *14 sts*

Next row (WS): Purl.

Next row: Knit to last 4 sts, k2tog, k2. *13 sts*

Rep last 2 rows four (three:three) times more. *9 (10:10) sts*

Cont straight until front matches Back to start of shoulder shaping, ending after a purl row.

Shape shoulder

Cast off rem 9 (10:10) sts.

Return to sts left on holder and slip centre 2 sts onto a safety pin. Rejoin appropriate yarn to rem sts with RS facing and cont as follows:-

Row 1 (RS): K2, skpo, knit to last 4 sts, k2tog, k2.

Row 2: Purl.

Row 3: K2, skpo, knit to last 4 sts, k2tog, k2. *18 (20:22) sts*

Rep rows 2 and 3 two (three:four) times more. *14 sts*

Next row (WS): Purl.

Next row: K2, skpo, knit to end. *13 sts*

Rep last 2 rows four (three:three) times more. *9 (10:10) sts*

Cont straight until front matches Back to start of shoulder shaping, ending after a knit row.

Shape shoulder

Cast off rem 9 (10:10) sts.

Neckband

Join right shoulder seam.

With 3.75mm needles and A, pick up and knit 32 (32:36) sts down left side of neck, knit 2 sts left on safety pin placing a marker on needle between these 2 sts, pick up and knit 32 (32:34) sts up right side of neck, then knit across 20 (20:22) sts on back holder. *86 (86:94) sts*

Row 1 (WS): P2, [k2, p2] rep to end.

This row sets position of rib.

Keeping rib correct, cont as follows:-

Row 2: Rib to within 2 sts of marker, k2tog, slip marker onto right needle, skpo, rib to end. *84 (84:92) sts*

Row 3: Rib to within 1 st of marker, p2 (marker is between these 2 sts), rib to end. Rep rows 2 and 3 once more. *82 (82:90) sts* Cast off in rib, decreasing either side of marker as before.

Armbands

Join left shoulder and Neckband seam.

With 3.75mm needles and A, pick up and knit 62 (66:70) sts evenly all round armhole edge. Starting with row 2, work in rib as given for Back for 5 rows.

Cast off in rib.

To make up

Press carefully following instructions on ball band. Join side and Armhole Border seams, taking care to match stripes.

Garden Journal

A fantastic hand-made journal is a beautiful gift for a gardener. Have fun personalizing it and making it into a unique gift. We have used oilcloth to cover the journal, which is widely available in fabric shops. It can be wiped down and is waterproof, which is handy when the journal is being dragged around a muddy garden. There is also a seed pocket on the inside to keep seeds handy.

Garden Journal

Size

A5 (210 x 148mm/8¼ x 5⅞in)

Materials

- 50cm (20in) oilcloth or waxed paper
- A5 ring binder
- All purpose extra-strong clear adhesive
- Seed packets
- A5 sheets of hand-made paper or parchment
- Hole punch
- Acrylic paints
- Artist's paintbrush
- A5 sheets of white quality paper (140/150gsm)
- Decorative sheets of paper or wrapping paper
- Paper flowers for front cover

Covering the journal

Place the oilcloth or waxed paper wrong side facing up. Open the folder flat and place it in the centre of the oilcloth. Measure the distance from the bottom end of the ring binder strip to the bottom of the folder. Measure the same distance down from the bottom edge of the folder, mark on the oilcloth. Repeat at the top.

Measure the distance from the fold line of the spine to the outer edge of the folder. Measure the same distance out from the edge of the folder and mark on the oilcloth. Repeat at the other side. Draw parallel lines through the marks to make an oblong. Cut the oilcloth to this size.

Cut across the corners diagonally. Centre the folder on the oilcloth. Glue and fold the top and bottom edges over the folder. Place a dry cloth over the oilcloth and press firmly with an iron. Glue and fold the sides in place, place a dry cloth over the oilcloth and press firmly.

Seed pocket

Measure the size of a pocket to take seed packets on the inside front flap of the folder..

Add 1.5cm (²/₃in) to the measurements on each side and the bottom, then cut a piece of oilcloth to this size. Fold a 1.5cm (²/₃in) hem on the sides and bottom and either glue or sew in place. Glue the pocket onto the folder.

Insert seed packets.

Season dividers

Take four sheets of the A5 paper or parchment and make holes with a punch so they will fit into the binder. Paint or draw fruit, vegetables or flowers for Spring, Summer, Autumn and Winter. In our journal we have used flowers for Spring, cherries and raspberries for Summer, apples for Autumn and frosty leaves and pine cones for Winter. If you don't feel confident painting or drawing, cut out pictures from magazines or look online at scrapbooking websites for ideas.

Inserting paper and decorating

Fill in between the parchment season dividers with good quality white A5 paper for notes on planting, garden plans, vegetable schedules and timetables.

You can also cut up wrapping paper or decorative paper to fit into the journal, to make further dividers.

Finally, glue a spray of paper flowers to the front cover to decorate.

A personalized garden journal will make a unique and welcome gift for a keen gardener.

Mosaic Plaque

Breaking up crockery is a very satisfying activity and this mosaic couldn't be easier. Start collecting any old broken or chipped china that you just can't bear to throw away. This plaque makes such a pretty gift and looks very impressive, but it costs very little and takes only a few hours to make. Make the recipient's initial, or a number plaque for their home.

Mosaic Plaque

Size
Approx 30 x 30cm (12 x 12in)

Materials
- 30cm (12in) square piece of 12mm (¼in) thick MDF
- PVA glue
- 3–5 china tea plates
- Small pot of strong white tile adhesive
- Limestone grout in a colour of your choice

Tools
- Jigsaw
- Paintbrush
- Protective glasses
- Assortment of cloths
- Small hammer
- Small flat knife or artist's palette
- Knife
- Sponges
- Paint
- 'D' ring (optional)

1) Trace a letter or number onto the piece of MDF – or, if you prefer, a shape such as a heart or a square. Try printing a letter from a computer and trace around it.

2) Cut the letter out using an electric jigsaw. If you are not confident using a power tool, take a template of your letter to your local timber merchant and they will cut it for you.

3) Using a paintbrush, apply a thin coat of PVA glue to one side of the shape. Allow to dry for approx 10–15 minutes.

4) Meanwhile, take the pieces of crockery and put one plate at a time inside a tea towel or large cloth. Wearing protective glasses, to avoid any chips going into your eyes, smash the plate with the hammer into small pieces approx 1–2cm (2/3–3/4in) in length.

5) Using a flat knife or palette knife, spread the tile adhesive onto small areas of the shape at a time. Lay the broken crockery one piece at a time onto the adhesive, leaving a small gap in between each one.

6) When the whole piece is completed, set aside for approx 20 minutes. As the adhesive starts to set, pick off any excess and leave the piece to dry according to the manufacturer's instructions on the pot.

7) Mix the grout according to the instructions on the packet. Using a palette knife and the tips of your fingers, spread it between the gaps of the crockery, working it in thoroughly. Be careful not to cut yourself on any sharp edges of china.

8) With a dry sponge, wipe the excess grout off the face of the tiles. Tidy up the edges by pushing the grout into the gaps and away from the tile faces. Leave to dry for approx 15 minutes.

9) Using a damp sponge, wipe as much of the excess grout off the tiles as possible. Set aside for 5 minutes. Wipe off excess grout two or three more times until the crockery is standing out clearly without any grout smudges.

10) When the grout is completely dry, shine up the crockery with a duster.

11) Paint the sides of the wood with a contrasting colour and fix a 'D' ring at the back to hang the shape if required.

Shopper

This bag is not only a fantastic shopping bag, but can also be used as a book bag for children, a vegetable bag, a swimming bag, a laundry bag – anything. It's also reversible, so if you get bored with one design then simply turn it inside out and use the other side. Within just an hour or two you will have transformed a simple piece of fabric into something inspiring. Once you have made one, you'll realize just how easy it is and you'll be making more bags for all your friends and family.

Shopper

Size

Finished measurement: 36cm (14¼in) wide and 39.5cm (16in) long With 1.5cm (⅔in) side and bottom seams and 5cm (2in) seam allowance at the top

Materials

- 75cm (30in) of 90cm (36in) wide main fabric
- 75cm (30in) of 90cm (36in) wide contrast lining fabric
- Sewing needle
- Thread to match fabric

Tip

Press all seams open after sewing.

1) Measure and cut two 39 x 46cm (15¾ x 17¼in) pieces in both the main fabric and the lining fabric.

2) Using the main fabric, pin the back and front pieces together with right sides together. Sew with a straight stitch down two sides and across the bottom with a 1.5cm (⅔in) seam allowance. Remove the pins.

3) Repeat step 2 with the two pieces of lining fabric.

4) Cut seams diagonally across the two bottom corners of both lining and main fabric, being very careful not to cut into the stitches.

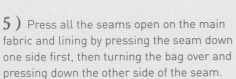

5) Press all the seams open on the main fabric and lining by pressing the seam down one side first, then turning the bag over and pressing down the other side of the seam.

6) Turn the main fabric bag right side out, making sure the corners are neat and square.

7) Put your hand inside the lining fabric bag and slip the main fabric bag over the top, smoothing the creases and easing the two layers together. Make sure that the lining fabric is thoroughly inside the main bag.

8) Measure 33cm (13in) from the bottom of the bag and place a marker pin in three places along the top, on each side of the bag.

9) Turn under the main fabric at marker points, press and then take out the marker pins. Pin the folded-over top in place ready for sewing.

10) Fold the lining fabric inside to meet the fold on the top of the main fabric bag, making sure that the lining and the main fabric are exactly the same height. Press in place.

11) Cut two strips 58 x 6cm (23 x 2½in) from both the lining fabric and the main fabric. On one of the lining fabric strips, fold over by a quarter of the width down the entire length of the strip. Press in place, then repeat on the other side of the strip.

12) Repeat with the other lining fabric strip and both main fabric strips.

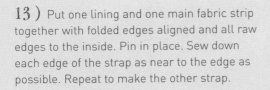

13) Put one lining and one main fabric strip together with folded edges aligned and all raw edges to the inside. Pin in place. Sew down each edge of the strap as near to the edge as possible. Repeat to make the other strap.

14) Slide the ends of one of the straps between the lining and the main fabric on one side of the bag. Each end of the strap should be positioned 8cm (3¼in) from the side seam of the bag. Pin in place.

15) Turn the bag over and insert the other strap in the same way, making sure it is exactly the same distance from the side seams as the strap on the other side. Pin so that both bag handles are an equal length.

16) Sew around the top edge of the bag, catching the ends of the straps as you sew. Use the edge of the machine foot as your width marker. Press.

17) Sew a small hand stitch in the bottom corners of the bag, so that when you reverse or wash it, the two fabric layers will stay together.

Man's Crochet Beanie

Making presents for men can sometimes be a challenge, but this crochet beanie has to be the most popular of all presents to give to a man – especially in winter months. Quick to make and using basic crochet stitches, this hat can be made in just one or two evenings and you can make it with stripes or in just one colourway. It takes very little yarn but be sure to use a soft, natural yarn for optimum comfort and warmth.

Man's Crochet Beanie

Size
Width around head 57cm (22½in)

Materials
- One 50g ball of Rowan Classic Cashsoft DK in each of Opulence 521 (A), Lichen 523 (B) and Savannah 507 (D)
- One 4.50mm crochet hook

Tension
17½ stitches and 15 rows to 10cm (4in) over half treble using 4.50mm crochet hook

Abbreviations
Ch:	chain
Cont:	continue
Dc:	double crochet
Htr:	half treble
Htr2tog:	[yarn over hook and insert hook as indicated, yarn over hook and draw loop through] twice, yarn over hook and draw through all five loops on hook
Ss:	slip stitch
St(s):	stitch(es)

Hat

With A, make 100 ch and join with a ss to form a ring, taking care to ensure ch is not twisted.

Round 1 (RS): 1 ch (does NOT count as st), 1 dc into each ch to end, ss to first dc. *100 sts*

Round 2: 1 ch (does NOT count as st), 1 dc into each dc to end, ss to first dc.

Using A, work in dc for 1 round more.

Join in B.

Using B, work in dc for 3 rounds.

Join in C.

Using C, work in dc for 3 rounds.

Round 10: Using A, 2 ch (counts as first htr), miss st at base of 2 ch, 1 htr into each st to end, ss to top of 2 ch at beg of round.

Using A, work in htr for 1 round more.

Using B, work in htr for 2 rounds.

Using C, work in htr for 2 rounds.

Last 6 rounds form stripe.

Keeping stripes correct as now set, cont in striped htr as follows:-

Work 2 rounds.

Round 18: 2 ch (counts as first htr), miss st at base of 2 ch, [htr2tog over next 2 htr, 1 htr into each of next 7 htr] eleven times, ss to top of 2 ch at beg of round. *89 sts*

Work 1 round.

Round 20: 2 ch (counts as first htr), miss st at base of 2 ch, [htr2tog over next 2 htr, 1 htr into each of next 6 htr] eleven times, ss to top of 2 ch at beg of round. *78 sts*

Work 1 round.

Round 22: 2 ch (counts as first htr), miss st at base of 2 ch, [htr2tog over next 2 htr, 1 htr into each of next 5 htr] eleven times, ss to top of 2 ch at beg of round. *67 sts*

Work 1 round.

Round 24: 2 ch (counts as first htr), miss st at base of 2 ch, [htr2tog over next 2 htr, 1 htr into each of next 4 htr] eleven times, ss to top of 2 ch at beg of round. *56 sts*

Round 25: 2 ch (counts as first htr), miss st at base of 2 ch, [htr2tog over next 2 sts, 1 htr into each of next 3 htr] eleven times, ss to top of 2 ch at beg of round. *45 sts*

Round 26: 2 ch (counts as first htr), miss st at base of 2 ch, [htr2tog over next 2 sts, 1 htr into each of next 2 htr] eleven times, ss to top of 2 ch at beg of round. *34 sts*

Round 27: 2 ch (counts as first htr), miss st at base of 2 ch, [htr2tog over next 2 sts, 1 htr into next htr] eleven times, ss to top of 2 ch at beg of round. *23 sts*

Round 28: 2 ch (counts as first htr), miss st at base of 2 ch, [htr2tog over next 2 sts] eleven times, ss to top of 2 ch at beg of round. *12 sts*

Fasten off.

To make up

Run a gathering thread around top of last round and pull up tight to close top of hat. Fasten off securely.

Knitting

Knit Stitch

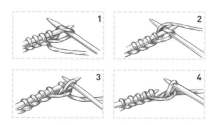

1) Hold the needle with the cast-on stitches in your left hand, with the loose yarn at the back of the work. Insert the right-hand needle from front to back of the first stitch on the left-hand needle.
2) Wind the yarn from left to right over the point of the right-hand needle.
3) Draw the yarn through the stitch, thus forming a new stitch on right-hand needle.
4) Slip the original stitch off the left-hand needle, keeping the new stitch on the right-hand needle.
5) To knit a row, repeat steps 1 to 4 until all the stitches have been transferred from the left-hand needle to the right-hand needle. Turn the work, transferring the needle with the stitches to your left hand to work the next row.

Purl

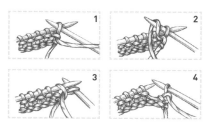

1) Hold the needle with the stitches in your left hand with the loose yarn at the front of the work. Insert the right-hand needle from back to front of the first stitch on the left-hand needle.
2) Wind the yarn from right to left over the point of the right-hand needle.
3) Draw the yarn through the stitch, thus forming a new stitch on the right-hand needle.
4) Slip the original stitch off the left-hand needle, keeping the new stitch on the right-hand needle.
5) To purl a row, repeat steps 1 to 4 until all the stitches have been transferred from the left-hand needle to the right-hand needle. Turn the work, transferring the needle with the stitches to your left hand to work the next row.

Increasing

The simplest method of increasing one stitch is to work into the front and back of the same stitch.

On a knit row, knit into the front of the stitch to be increased, then before slipping it off the needle, place the right-hand needle behind the left-hand needle and knit again into the back of the same stitch. Slip the original stitch off the left-hand needle.

On a purl row, purl into the front of the stitch to be increased, then before slipping it off the needle, purl again into the back of the same stitch. Slip the original stitch off the left-hand needle.

Decreasing

The simplest method of decreasing one stitch is to work two stitches together. On a knit row, insert the right-hand needle from front to back through two stitches instead of one, then knit them together as one stitch. This is called knit two together (k2tog).

On a purl row, insert the right-hand needle from back to front through two stitches instead of one, then purl them together as one stitch. This is called purl two together (p2tog).

Embroidery Stitches

Crochet Stitches

Satin Stitch
French Knot

Slip Knot
Chain Stitch

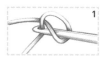

Satin Stitch

French Knot

Slip Knot

1) Almost all crochet begins with a slip knot. Make a loop, then hook another loop through it. Tighten gently and slide the knot up to the hook.

Chain Stitch

1) Yarn over and draw the yarn through to form a new loop without tightening up the previous one.

2) Repeat to form as many chains as required. Do not count the slip knot as a stitch. Note: Unless otherwise stated, when working into the starting chain always work under two strands of chain loops as shown in the following diagrams.

Double Crochet, Half Treble, Treble

Double crochet

 1
 2

Half treble

 1
 2
 3
 4

Treble

 1
 2
 3
 4
 5

Double Crochet

1) Insert the hook into the work (second chain from hook on starting chain), *yarn over and draw yarn through the work only.
2) Yarn over again and draw the yarn through both loops on the hook.
3) 1dc made. Insert hook into next stitch; repeat from * in step 1.

Half Treble

1) Yarn over and insert the hook into the work (third chain from hook on starting chain).
2) *Yarn over and draw through the work only.
3) Yarn over again and draw through all three loops on the hook.
4) 1hdc made. Yarn over, insert the hook into the next stitch; repeat from * in step 2.

Treble

1) Yarn over and insert the hook into the work (fourth chain from hook on starting chain).
2) *Yarn over and draw through the work only.
3) Yarn over and draw through the first two loops only.
4) Yarn over and draw through the last two loops on the hook.
5) 1dc made. Yarn over, insert hook into next stitch; repeat from* in step 2.

Acknowledgements

A big thanks to Andy and Johnny at Laughing Hens for generously donating so much of their Rooster Yarn for the knitted and crochet items; to Caroline Cowan, Tracey Elks and Liz Colquitt for all their help; to Roger Perkins who always puts things in the right place; to my mum, Beryl, for showing me how to discover the joy of making my own gifts; to my daughters, Camilla and Maddy, for continuing the family dynasty and contributing their talents to almost every project in the book. And finally, thanks to Miriam Hyslop and everyone at Anova Books for making the book happen.

Photography by Holly Jolliffe.

Love crafts?

Crafters... keep updated on all
exciting craft news from Collins & Brown.
Email **lovecrafts@anovabooks.com** to
register for free email alerts on
forthcoming titles and author events.